Sights, Sounds, and Spirit

Collected Poems 1990-2015

by David A. Folds

WingSpan Press

Published in the United States and the United Kingdom
by WingSpan Press, Livermore, CA

The WingSpan name, logo and colophon are
the trademarks of WingSpan Publishing.

ISBN 978-1-59594-581-5

First edition 2016

Printed in the United States of America

www.wingspanpress.com

Library of Congress Control Number 2016932964

1 2 3 4 5 6 7 8 9 10

SIGHTS, SOUNDS, AND SPIRIT

THIS IS DEDICATED
TO MY WIFE, VICKIE,
AND MY BROTHER, CHUCK.

Status Quo

this is now the game

what is love

each time asking

do you love me

knowing but asking

to hear

the words

again the same unless

I fool her and

answer wrong but

still she knows but

must hear

again the same

this time that

still I do

1990 - NYC

David A. Folds

To Sophia

Standing simply

Start in silence

Opening outward

Drop to daylight

Lift the lightness

Enter the eternal

Holding delicately the hollow of wholeness.

Fast to focus

Flow to form

Cut through currents

Curve through clouds

Soft but solid

Biased and balanced

Floating on lofty and rooted limbs.

My chi is glowing

My mind is focused

On flowing, slicing fingertips

But Sophia sighs

Pauses a moment

Oh, you've lost it. ..... Let's start again.

9/22/96 - NYC

3

David A. Folds

Reflecting Pool

Listen in silence

to silence

as the day brokers itself

towards its own demise

Passing in the quiet of the

thunder of bustling hives

thought, as daylight, flits about

among the flowers of experiences

and the dung-heaps of our recognition

to find once, perhaps, everything

in a bell, nectar-rich,

giving presence and focus

to the silence that swims

slithering through our springs

and summers before our

fall to our own

pool of reflection

into winter -- is it ice or glass?

reflecting the vastness of the

space above   from the chilled

dungeon below the glass

we will pause for ages   wondering

5/23/1997 - NYC

David A. Folds

Long Notes

Don't sing it, baby, listen to these blues.

The rain knows more than you or I do.

Drops float like notes

and are gone ....

spread out, at landing,

over everywhere.

Dampness .... humidity clings

to flesh

and now deeper

through to bones.

Darkness overhead,

clouds menace and

explode .... a shower

of more than gloom.

-- there is no light.

Darkness dropped down

to dampness,

no-one arrived at nowhere,

nothing to be seen or felt,

But the song has a beginning,

know that

and find an end.

Blues walked in, and now be gone again.

6/7/1997 - NYC

David A. Folds

Sounds of Change

Listen to the sounds,

Movement in the trees,

Leaves vibrate in the wind,

A chorus announcing in agreement,

Change .... coming soon,

Coming now.

Listen in the woods.

The sounds are always full,

Sometimes softly,

Sometimes not.

Sounds of change are always heard,

Sometimes loudly,

Sometimes not.

6/25/1997 - NYC

Enter Ideas

the largeness of small

plays the pulse of inbetweens

the motion of midnight

waves towards its own repeal

lastly a common thought

bursts through to dominate

laughing its triumph

over my brief escape

from life

from prison

from death

from me

4/8/1997- NYC

9

David A. Folds

Duet

Lightning rod to my soul,

it seems

that even the smallest

acts --- gestures --- emotions

draw focus

when I open my senses,

which is not always,

but enough

to continue cementing

a connection,

often quiet above, but,

underneath --- unseen --- unheard,

sinews of union

straddle the space between

and We continue.

10/4/1997 - NYC

Now's Revenge

It was the last of the last of the last

before the first of the last.

The long sighing of silence

-- time bent out of shape --

Today should not still be here.

Each tick like before and after,

like every other tock,

like every pause between a

tick tock tick.

Where is the change?

My time is not now, not yet,

but my time must be now, or soon.

I grow old waiting for my time.

But what is time, my time,

but the waiting and trying

and doing and the surprise

and wonder of joy and pain.

12/6/1997 - NYC

David A. Folds

All Light

Into the breach goes nothing.

Now…illusions of life

…shadow-dances on a wall…

an all-encompassing universe,

dissipate, like drying mist.

Our patterns are games of light

drawn from

a kaleidoscope's random choices,

a few colors to make the game.

There---a beacon in the night,

   A pathway to the brilliance,

There...no rays explode like lightning,

   but envelop from without...within.

There...is a start,

   here at rainbow's end.

Once found, learn to exist

   where self disappears

   and nothing is everywhere.

12/16/1997 Tacloban,
Leyte, Philippines

David A. Folds

Dances of the Tribe

Passing the salt...

   We are conditioned

   from childhood...

Crossing at the green...

   to respond within

   restricted possibilities...

Don't play with your food...

   to dance within the

   group's moves and turns...

Parking here is not allowed...

   to act somewhat like our neighbors,

   but not (quite) the same.

Zip up, you're not finished…

    We waffle in and out of sync,

    as the impulses of self

    ebb and flow.

Your slip is showing…

    We think we are those small

    occasional steps outside the tribe,

    not the rest of the times…conforming.

You left the seat up…again.

12/18/1997 Tacloban,
Leyte, Philippines

David A. Folds

Diversions

Lost in time…

    wandering through

        the small rooms of life,

I stop at favorite furniture,

    rapt in concentration,

        in turn,

    in the experience of each

Until…

    no longer floating in details,

        the smallness flits away

            its specialness

like a wink somewhere

in the vastness of space,

not even noticed by

anyone...

anything.

And...my journey continues

past space

and time.

*12/20/1997 Tacloban,
Leyte, Philippines*

David A. Folds

Growth and Pain

We are…

      the true locusts of the world,

spread across the splotched land

in the breadth of the careless cities,

consuming all that we can

      of the earth's exposures,

      without finishing the deeds

         …closing the doors.

We leave tortured reminders

      of our orgies of experience

      in the ruts and spendings,

strewn through our recent

      and current paths

         …with no remorse.

No respect for the land is a curse.

But, not to respect the totality is worse.

We grow at the cost of all that we use,

   …we and it are changed

   …neither ever again to be the same.

*12/22/1997, Tacloban,
Leyte, Philippines*

19   David A. Folds

Cheap Elevations

Lofty is small.

Wealth is wide, but small.

Always wishing to elevate awareness

or recognition

or desiring to amass more,

fills our usually hopeless dreams.

You gain through work or luck.

Flowers growing what you sow,

but sometimes,

a random wind or

a carrier on wings

drops

a seed somewhere

and from it

grows something

from no work of yours.

And its wealth spreads to you

and esteem follows

like a lapdog

and you enjoy the harvest.

But, you must know who

is you.

6/22/1998
NY, NY

David A. Folds

Minuscule

Let it go!

Tresses of tentacles from the mind

grasp at what the mind

cannot imagine releasing

It is as though this…

some small connection

…some identification

is the thing that defines

our entire being

Focusing on this microcosm

ignoring the vastness of our own

much larger macrocosm

to say nothing of the

infinite vastness

of all existence

We sit in our chosen life-raft

    floating in a sea

        of possibilities we ignore

Holding on to this...

    we lose much more

Let it go!

12/13/1999 Tacloban,
Leyte, Philippines

23

David A. Folds

Out of the Dark

Out of dark sleep

    drift images floating in

    and out of logic

    superimposed moments of

    under-currents of thought

    trying...trying to tell...

    until they do not so much stop

        as evolve into the

            beginnings of morning

Now, morning warps slowly in an ellipse

    toward awakened awareness

But at the end of the ellipse

    comes a dull thud

Yes...awake

    ...but nothing is working yet

No beacon shows the way

    only past memory of

        morning rituals acts as usher

So, follow the same rutted path

    the sure, boring pattern

Unaware of a kaleidoscope of options

Making progress...supposedly

Preparing...

Each segment with

    its sequences and timings

Each performed the same as before

    only minimally focused

Not so much aware elsewhere

    as not there...

        with that segment

        ...nor the next...or the next

Somewhere in a half-world of awareness

    while existence all around bursts in fullness

Probably...perhaps

David A. Folds

We break out from the mother

...from the walls that embrace

in the moment of change

...from home...less ready

than pushed by time

...by schedules

pre-planned paths

with mini-milestones

but without rhythm...each

step rushed to reach

our own...outside

Sunlight strikes our skin

like the doctor's slap

...a jolt that forces

re-adjustment

Standing in the brightness

...for a moment

we begin to refocus

Striding with direction

toward resurrection

...toward servitude

Quickly...

Walk down in darkness

lightened for your safety

...dingy for your comfort

Pay out the morning tribute

entering to share a journey

Wait in clumps...

close to the chasm

Look left for light

...beacons beginning

Waiting for...not yours...but

a train's phantom timetable

David A. Folds

With all but the heat

    of a dragon's breath,

Wind blasts through the

    commuting crowd

The roar rumbling in

    advance of a parade of

    stained steel-boxed bullies

Even the numbing dull-decibel

    thrust does not

    convey the power

    passing and slowly

    decelerating...towards a stop

    Each eye watches cars

    pass...measuring how

    full...how empty

Is there room?...any seats at all?

Wishing...waiting for a full stop

...for jaws to gape open

to engulf those willing

to enter quickly

between close-standing crowds

outside and in and

past a reverse rush

pushing to escape

Once inside...

find a place...

not a haven or a home

...more a refuge

in a moving bunker

David A. Folds

Shaken…rattling

reverberating from some

external explosion

that never culminates

but continues creating

controlled havoc

Until each station stop

provides a respite

from one harassment

replaced by another…

neighbors determined to detrain

Followed by renewed

tyranic movement

…motivated forward

hopefully

…until your own escape

Lost in a moment...

a spark of freedom

felt in the open air

of the closed city

out from the tube

bringing life

...violently

You are just one more

corpuscle...

seeking the path to a

dna-assigned task

Fate controls...

continues to link

phases...

particles of a

larger continuum

...controlling

David A. Folds

Now…take your places

…please

Walk quickly to the building

…the job

…your cubicle

12/13/1999 Tacloban,
Leyte, Philippines

Eternal Moments

into sharp silence bursts

a dull sound

into dark twilight emerges

a new dawn

lifetimes are dances

-- until discarded

worries will hide

and snicker

but, breathing pulses

below calmness

with passion's lower

half ignored

the rest expands and rises

-- floating in, but never

recognizing

a sea that will never end

5/9/2000 - NYC

David A. Folds

Dawning Dusk

Long ago ... daylight was born

-- reincarnate – a new awareness

splashed on my face ... while,

trying to hide – enclosed in

my cocoon ... protection fading

(partial can be fatal)

Not so long ago ... moonlight was born

I had grown used to the daylight

now, no warm ray's bite,

now, no intensity of purpose,

only the coolness of patient calm,

is near

Echoes of the daylight still appear

sometimes invading

the rhythms of moonlight

sometimes mixing a cocktail

of feelings

that breach the gap between

the innocence of experience

and dullness of the senses

2000 - NYC, NY

David A. Folds

In Fellowship

In a sea among others

often there is a ...

separation ... loneliness

that closes communication

shutting down

chances for

synaptic whispers

until ...

the touch of laughter

vibrates ... through to skin

whether friendly or not

some embarrasses

some may shame

but, … what carries the tag

"join me"

sweeps me up

in a continuation of

its self-refreshing pulse

rhythm echoing still

well after it has gone

12/25/2000 Tacloban,
Leyte, Philippines

David A. Folds

Returning

I walk into

    a pool of mystery

    washing clean

        all understanding

    every concept drowns to

        disintegration

    connections losing all

        character

    less severed than vanished

I walk with no strides

    on no legs moving through

        no space wrapped in nothing

        with no curiosity

all is not dark,

    but blank

    moving with stillness

    with no motion

    radiating inward

    … outward, until

    the eyes choose something

        popping open

1/10/2001 Narita Airport,
Tokyo, Japan

David A. Folds

Sparrow

Songs of a sparrow -- float about

    from grass to bush to tree.

She nests, but rarely flies

    high where wings could draft and dip.

The earth, the bits and pieces gathered,

    sculpted to a home ... ground her.

By choice, do you say?

    There is none, she sees no other way.

Watch the clouds sweep in,

    soft blue turned white ... to gray.

Her nest, her surrounding world,

    balanced, in tune with beauty,

    her quiet grace, given to these goals,

    fills space between the surges and ebbs

    around her, the egos and the needs.

Thick clouds burst rain, flooding the tepid air,

coarse texture loading lungs like lead.

Still, her message is simple, but subdued:

prosper, with intelligence be kind,

and if you have the time,

will you remember me.

5/3/2001 New York
NY, USA

41   David A. Folds

Nibbling Time

I have felt the taste of Time.

Do I consume it or does it eat me?

The rush for higher conscience may

    seek to have an answer

    at the last gate's moment

    attaining a finish, embracing,

    enveloping Eternity.

But, will fate take your time?

Will your time tick off each second

towards a tape broken with finality,

or will moments accumulate, a symphony,

    adding more and more strings,

    swarming into a sound that

    radiates into every corner,

or will your growth more quietly build,

      stepping softly towards each experience?

Your journey, your hills and valleys,

      form the reply.

 Walk on, continue,

      even when you sit in silence,

for Time, every moment is a piece

      of the puzzle of Eternity.

6/18/2001 NYC

David A. Folds

Old Seasons

past life warped

      to present dreams

      floats in and

         out of focus

an amalgam

      of perceptions

      coloring the environment

         of awareness

flowers grow to bursting

      sensually...

      and then, spent,

      wither

      ...with licentiousness

      only as a memory

here, the remaining stripped

    stalwart stalks

    stand attention

    awaiting

    the iced entrance

       of winter

my boots step through them

    straddling to hardened turf

    pretending that nothing

    is changed

    …not the sod,

    the plants, the season, the person

only the breath, released,

    exits encased in mist

    proclaiming frigid times

…a tax on all our patience

David A. Folds

steps crunch dried earth

awaiting the onset

of a blanket...soft,

but transforming into ice

at first a covering...

pristine, undiluted,

dominant

later an environ

of trampling and pollution

later still a melting

to muddied paths

...slippery access only

boots exhausted

by a season

of rasping weather

still hope

for sustained cohesion

til they in turn

are stashed in storage

a sign that Spring

following its cue

has finally begun

and our stalks and roots

have survived...

older...a little drier,

a bit less able

to respond

with resilience

but still,

objects floating

in the continuum

...bravely we step forward

12/21/2001 Tacloban,
Leyte, Philippines

David A. Folds

Rebirth

From my window

    hushed morning

        climbs to power

            in an explosion of gold

       radiant heat

         expansive breathing

       slept awareness

         unfolding

my minds uncoils

    slowly … like an

       awakened cat

         ready to act, but

        not knowing to what

blues and grays are past

    oranges … yet to come

the soup is stirred

    yet who will eat it, when?

I am becoming,

    yet, again

6/30/02 - Jersey City, NJ

David A. Folds

Watching Time

Float the images

of dance

in a bottle

Wrap all gifts

to perfection

Turn today

into magic

not stepping in any

of the refuse

of life

Wish ... this escape

towards always

knowing ... it closer to

... never

What have we

without it?

Only to

breath in

… expand

watching … the second hand

race onward

7/10/02 - Jersey City, NJ

David A. Folds

Showers

It is a summer

    afternoon sudden rain

    wrapped around the edge of quiet

      … appearing dominant

    sweeping all the insignificant objects

      dripping clean … wind throwing

        water descending

My umbrella defender deciding

    to not be destroyed

    blasted by gusts

      with no answers

      … only questions

      … changing quickly

We are made instantly small

    not controlling … only reacting

hoping the onslaught

    only a short interruption

from our important indulgences

deciding to tolerate this

    rude indelicate downpour

7/12/02 - Jersey City, NJ

53

David A. Folds

Morning Journey

lasting

      into cold silence

I wish for dawn

        of new light

yellow...crawling forward

            ...til

     exploding into control

        ...dominant

the strength of daylight

     filling sinew with hope

     washes through resistance

flooding the senses

        ...bursting

     through closed doors

saturating

      darkened corners

set up the sail

sit

under the large umbrella

regaining control…we are

ready for today's voyage

12/31/02 - Mekong River near
Luang Prabang,

David A. Folds

Moments

after the slight sound

of sad laughter

moments dissipate

life paused ... while the

world spins ... I am

once again in continual

transition ...

so hard to define

what was before or

what next to be targeted

... if anything is still

approached ...

or gained or lost

where life exists

      change is always

... take a quick-shot

      imprison a moment

... still metamorphosis

      goes on and on ...

but do you know the

      many millions of moments

or do they pass unnoticed

      ... wind flying past you?

8/15/03 - Jersey City, NJ, USA

David A. Folds

River

I have walked through

the waters of my time

sloshing aimlessly

displacing bucket-loads

changing nothing ... the flow

of time continuing

seemingly unaffected

when by chance ... or focus

integrating my rhythm with

the forces of existence ... I am

magnetically balanced ... for

a moment I am complete

... not a fish doomed to

fight the current

cursed to travel in

opposition

... out of synch and time

awakened winds

rustle through trees ... bushes stirred

violently protesting

... softness of purpose brushed aside

this time is the same ... like no other

we wash the life from our senses

hoping to succeed ... survive

how to find your place

... what's the proper spot?

in a flowing ... even raging

torrent of water

river of all things with

expanse beyond experience

how is it possible to not be over-whelmed

... a mote among the infinite

David A. Folds

I am the softness under the

skin the flesh that loses

shape, without its cover

unwrapped ... uncontrolled

undirected ... where to seek?

in what form and what measure

what am I without

definition ... or with it?

if I know who I am ... I have lost

if I lose who I am ... I am found

to break the bonds of boundaries

to drop time, ruler of the finite

pass space and form

the tyrants ... to step

... beyond

10/05/03 - Jersey City, NJ, USA

Moment in Mount Laurel

the force of the flock

seems to overcome all

-- a vector of geese

plunging forward into

space – slicing the moment

each one determined to

stay with its position

each moment grabbing

new space --- territory gained

and instantly discarded

migration of

almost hysterical need

risen to a joy

of righteousness

and power

and chances of success

for a new generation

12/24/03 - Tacloban, Leyte, Philippines

David A. Folds

Lost in the Web

after the last joke has faded

   the quiet seeps through

   washing everything

   with relentless calm

old wounds throb …

   demanding

stirred from sleeping silence

   muffled sounds murmur

   beyond the closed door

   past the foreign corridor

   filling the vacuum with

    anonymous life

   an intruder with no

   conscience

thoughts return ...

regurgitated to stop the silence

nothing's new

no well's spring

    of ingenuity

no progress ...

a dog chasing its tail

the time has come to

    speak the words

    that gather focus

    that weave the web

    to link the moments

    that flit about

        unknowing, uncaring

    to a marriage

        of purpose

    wrapped around

    a weaver wishing to

        rebuild eternity

11/06/03 - Jersey City, NJ, USA

David A. Folds

Geodesic Oasis

when the wilted flowers

give up the ghost -- life ends

to begin again

when the warped reason

of civilization

reverses its ascending arc

peace can plunge

into a quiet grotto

-- an ill-fated respite

my mind seeks this quiet

when it remembers the need

the calm cooled-down flow

of caressing waters

envelops my consciousness

-- not numbing it

-- but surrounding it like

a geodesic dome

now peace has come

... until the bubble bursts

12/15/03 - Koh Sammui, Thailand

David A. Folds

Hiatus

in the canvas of laughter

ghosts float ... aimlessly

wrapped in some cataclysmic

reaction born of a

need for

lost imbalance

is it more prized

than peace?

what strength is gained

from cathartic interruption?

perhaps it briefly

washes from us

all doubts and fears

erases the focus on

all negatives ...

for a short time

until our memory ...

ultimately stronger

brings them back

relentlessly to focus

12/26/2004
Tacloban, Leyte, Philippines

David A. Folds

Perception

willows of the world

       laugh at supposed sorrows

morning glories weep

       helplessly

all imbalance placed

       in alignment

we set forth on a

       new day's confusion

barriers blockade the

       outside onslaught

at most ... drastic filtration

       seeps through

          softened reality

truth like unprocessed ore

       lacks refining and

       is surely unacceptable

we try to carve

a structured view

while truth fails to

wrap us in its reality

we are fanatic sculptors

defining the

art of our world

01/06/2005
Tacloban, Leyte, Philippines

David A. Folds

Passage

when everything's aligned

the soft measure

of truth

slips through the cracks

like melted butter

the proof that balances

… unravels

like an awakened snake

day's new light creeps

forward

… continually

gaining new ground

that cannot escape

until it seeks its

    own demise

... light slipping

    through the cracks

dripping

    through grasping

        fingers ... losing

    still another day

6/1/05 - Jersey City, NJ

David A. Folds

Heat

what is the answer

to questions

when winds weep

for calm

the longer days

rule bright suns

... a convention of

thick indifference

wood throbs softly

while lightly cooked

pavement takes each

step seeking an

unfound change

around the next corner

promising some difference

but it's still the same thing

slightly shifted

the answers

popping up ... like the figures

in a shooting gallery

8/3/05 - Jersey City, NJ

David A. Folds

Ebb Tide

the last lights

    sing softly

    after a short

        burst of

            dramatic dusk

prelude to a calm

    forced upon us

the air

    becoming quiet

while we choose

    to cast away

        energy accumulated

        amid day's dramas

one deep

    long breath

then ... slowly

    slowly

    seeking ...

        ... finding moments of peace

8/4/05 - Jersey City, NJ

David A. Folds

Silence

when they send the softness

down from heaven

... hidden among the

brash

trumpeting

of fortune and fame

pockets of peace

can be discovered

that hold nothing

quietly

vibrating

rays of light

pulse flowing

inward and out

we wash

  our becomings

    both bonding

      and merged

    with the deepest

      breath

    wrapped in a blanket

  a child of the ages

8/27/05 - Medford Leas, NJ

David A. Folds

Microbe

Listen ...

the walls bear witness

... keeping each vibration

... contained within

every loud silence

ricochets

... corner to corner

before fading ...

momentumless

when smallness

is uninterrupted

minuteness is left to

stir the mix

we experience

moments ... unmasked

unchallenged

by greater energy

a microsecond's ... aria

do not blink

... already

it will be gone

10/31/05 - Jersey City, NJ

David A. Folds

Changes

When the winter came

the wind ruled the land

we moved from one

barren stretch

to yet another

a coldness rooted down

through stumbling feet

an unfriendly union

on an uncaring platform

the trees laughed

... our only witness

Somehow ...

we reached the sea

now more bold in motion

than this stoic, static land

it would embrace

... encompass us

Somehow we refuse

   … floating

     … perilously

    insignificant plaything

     … slightest parenthesis

    to an awesome current

Someday we woke

   and we were beached

  … warm sand

    tepid, lapping tide

the sun laughed …

   we stretched slowly

    … then, a stroll

   all in wonder

11/30/05 - Jersey City, NJ

81

David A. Folds

Two

love ...

    like glue

        stretched however far

        pulsates

        in various time

    captive to

        the mood of the moment

    the vectors of life

        compete with a

           shifting variety

           of directions

    muscles alternately

        flexed and then

           forgotten

our breath

     is held back

     stunned by

        its highest intensity

         occasionally

moments

     when we feel alone

     a subtle undercurrent

        strokes the quiet places

           in our mind

     like an old friend

        tapping on our shoulder

         from behind

     hello,

        yes … I'm still here

11/30/05 - Jersey City, NJ

David A. Folds

To the Core

in the earlier days

    we walked on Earth

    directly

in touch with the pulse

    of the mother

a line of communion

    passing

        from deepest core

our knowledge was small

    but connected

        and balanced

loneliness greeted

    the loss of Eden

confusion surrounded the steps

    of our learning

growing with the strength

    and the pain

power radiating outward

but not to our center

now we could be everywhere

... everywhere but here

still somewhere

in the quiet

of our oldest purpose

some seek the heart

of separation

to find the center

of the silence

that radiates

in totality

to the rhythm

of the universe

... come

12/13/05 - Isan, Thailand

85

David A. Folds

Lessons

while ambiguous Autumn

rules the sun

we sit in a

soft cold memory

of lessons

learned and lost

private thoughts

darting in and out

from ideas

floated in the air

occasionally caught

often only watched

passing seemingly

to nowhere

so many ideas

    rejected

    … not exciting

    … not useful, now

    … not presented

       dynamically

food never ingested

    with no solid substance

someplace

    they reside

       unwanted

orphans

    waiting for a choice

12/18/05 - Hua Hin, Thailand

David A. Folds

Old Isan

here ...

    the simple people live

      a life

      similar to those

      who came before

        three millennium ago

build up from the ground

    on stilts ... for safety

gather from the trees

    and the water

plant in the cleared

    soft earth

fish the stream

    hunt the forest

make pottery in clay

and metal ware

and glass

cook out of created pots

beget the child

who will follow

bury the ones

who gave back

their energy

to survive

remember them

in the heart

... some days

12/18/05 - Hua Hin, Thailand

David A. Folds

Sweeping By

I am the wind

swept high above the crowd

uncoiling and twisting

seeking

the quiet places

where everything

bends to my

insistent strength

the will to bend things ...

and the will to bend

... or to resist

matter becomes ...

choosing its character

finding purpose

... reason for structure

or amorphic

flexibility

everywhere below

    things appear

        stay ...

            or disappear

    while I move by

        watching and touching

12/31/05 - road to Hua Hin, Thailand

David A. Folds

Cosmic Breaths

the sun spoken

    in cosmic anger

    invades everything

        that's unprotected

heat pulsating

    ... vibrations

        per microsecond

the broad smile of life

    and death

the rain becomes

    a confessor

    washing everything

        that's unprotected

after the heat ...

    a full baptism

        water sustaining life

we walk on

seeking

newness

worried about

safety

the wind increases

... the beginnings

of cruelty

the drying force

taking from us

the liquid strength

wrapping around us

... unavoidable

connection

David A. Folds

the lightness of

early snow

tries to fool us

this is not our friend

... more

blankets of freezing snow

will follow

until ...

our lives are covered

enveloped

by cold embrace

... stop-freeze the body

... let the spirit escape

01/04/05 - road to Bangkok, Thailand

Light Years

the wax drips slowly

    reforming

        in layered clusters

strains of color

    separate

    creating

        impromptu

          patterns

time passes

    flying away

      quickly

      uncaring

moments move into

    months

years pass

    waiting for

      a next millennium

David A. Folds

you sigh, seeing

now …

now with little caring

the truth

as a tight formation

melts into

a seamless blot

the clock still ticks

… showing

the measured

certainty of time

but …

choose to look elsewhere

and time can

float away …

reach into

     the open air

     to grasp at ...

       nothing

the same nothing

     from moments before

        and millenniums back

       and more to come

        someday

01/11/06 - Bangkok, Thailand

David A. Folds

Dad – a Gift to Us

he was born and raised

to value

the moments

of life

a traveler

taking others

on journeys

of esthetic wealth

finding

ways to open

eyes and minds

to the heart

of the creative

spirits that

brought forth

visual vibrations

painted for the ages

when all was told

    it was about

        heart and beauty

there was no quota

    of kindness

it was spiritual

    ... growth in karmic tones

01/27/06 - bus from Medford Leas, NJ

David A. Folds

An Eye For Luck

the passion of peace

felt in the morning

... light-bleached moments

time stopped to quiet

fields of grass

... nearby water

life at a pause in Southbury

a foursome strolling

slowly ... for pleasure

my mother with special talent

passed down from

her mother

searching for another

four-leaf clover

Dad stopped again

    talking to someone or other

Vickie and I along with them

    observing ... absorbing

    smiling at almost everything

and then to our surprise

    among the so many common threes

    she did it ...

        she found yet another

03/28/06 - Jersey City, NJ

David A. Folds

Phases

sands of the desert

    trapped in arid death

    would wish for the wash

      of ocean's tides

a rebirth by baptism

    a chance to change

we live

    in the constant moments

we breath ... the dry air

    deserted by the cool waters

no new visions

    no corner turned

we welcome any warped

versions of yesterday

anything different

but, the difference

is still the same

and ... who knows that

the sameness is really

the only difference

04/03/06 - Jersey City, NJ

David A. Folds

On Stage

grey brown mist skims softly

over early morning dew

quiet broken by an occasional bird

... life awakened

but we ... mostly are not

yellow orange dawn

flirts with the horizons

silent drama

prelude to

the harsh bleached

glare of morning

... our play's true director

scenes forced

into the spot-light

time demanding …

… the actor's entrance

play the scene

improvise

all await the power of the sun …

words … a gesture with direction

05/12/06 - Jersey City, NJ

David A. Folds

Dark Dreams

I dreamed

    the sleeping sky

    thinking beige

        and maroon

    warped by

        androgynous tints

    closed all access

my breath, thick to clotting

    air compressed

my eyes

    held low

    below the squeezed

    horizon

captive to

      environmental tyranny

I wait for any respite

      a pause ... a reprieve

      ... some compassion

perhaps the clouds

      will open up

         ... exploding

      drenching all

      objects

but ... no response comes

      from pity

David A. Folds

waiting … waiting

for one mote

to emerge

a window of change

… life's river halted

until … until

… I awaken

with morning lights

growing

soft radiance

the pulse of life

is starting

in rhythm

07/10/06 - Jersey City, NJ

My Truth

wind whipped fiercely

    against a window

time still passing

thoughts floating and

    shifting

memories trying to emerge

filtered images dance

    against the force

        of a present that will

        not stop

        … not stay still

I am awash within a

    mental montage

… mixed past and present

    … reality holds

a painting

    of irregular

        perspective

12/05/06 - Jersey City, NJ

David A. Folds

Closed Doors

how have we lost the way?

... with clarity from

clouded conclusions

daybreak bursts through

spaced slats at a

window facing East

truth seeks a path

to recognition

passing outer defenses

reaches a blockade inside

that resists any

intrusive reality

outside the wind rushes by

... sounds of impatience

... seeking everything

and we just lost

another day

12/24/06 - Jersey City, NJ

David A. Folds

Darshan

the India of the Tamil south

wrapped in daily darshan

temples with vibrant images

of saints and gods

dancing, praying

meditating and glowing

the outer temple

caught in chaos

elephants blessing

stalls selling

beggars asking

… sometimes pleading

worshipers arush

towards their daily

morning bliss

all to reach a special focus

   … heightened moments

      of a special darshan

  holy ashes on top of ashes

    my shoulders

       blessed with garlands

  a broom wide swept overhead

    then a touch

       upon the seventh chakra

final word

  from a dramatic search

    for all the peace and balance

02/03/07 - Kovalam, Kerala, India

David A. Folds

Slow Waters

I have come to a time

without sorrow

emotions lying low

floating on a flat

line of progression

there is no touch of tragedy

… if there is

I do not feel it

the past washes over

with a sterile touch

the present hangs loosely

uncommitted

not searching through life's

shopping malls

wishing for nothing

no bargain of experience

prices reduced

I am not a customer

an immobile buoyancy

heightened moments

with no river current

… then I begin to swim

02/22/07 - Jersey City, NJ

David A. Folds

Fog

the moon glides south

quietly

the echo of silence

breeched, occasionally

a car or a

dog barking

... breathing life slowly

sleep provides the

space in between

the time that feels

like no time

dreams floating

... a patchwork

jigsaw puzzle

a montage

paints the landscape

breath quickens

then stopped

diaphragm filled

held so long, then

released like an

opened furnace

eyelids retreat

lens trying to focus

… the baked predawn

reality intrudes

knowing no better

we walk

unprepared into

a glazed

moment of awareness

05/29/07 - Jersey City, NJ

David A. Folds

Geese

let the blue gray banner

flutter

in the energy

of a trenchant wind

watch the calm motion

of Canadian geese

glide softly

on furrowed waters

with nutrients of promise

occasionally … head dipping

… tail raising

dining

close to people watching

… some ignoring

lost in the nature

of their unnaturalness

… a few quietly entwined

in the soft rhythm

of an old universe

a blessing in disguise

7/12/08 - Jersey City, NJ

David A. Folds

Raptor Rising

wings work a whirling whip like

scooping grasp of air

dropping down and repeated

and again

gaining lift -   rising into lofty

atmosphere

to reach altitudes with wide

spanning scope

eyes scanning all

the mottled surface

until a choice ...

a target ... is spotted

then – beak dropping, head aiming

wings pulled in tight ... flattened

to minimize resistance

... accelerating

toward one meal

and one death

2/20/13 - Jersey City, NJ

David A. Folds

Trips

... and so the begin starts to begin

time moving once again ... slowly

a step into a bright space

- sun-locked, heat-sparkled

moving forward

towards shade

glazed images streak through

parched atmosphere

my own lens closed

trying to avoid the onslaught

I float through it

an alien thrown into warped time

landing could have been

smoother

a few disruptive hops

then ... followed by

reverse engine ... stopping

slow, slower taxiing

faces turned to relief

    tired but half at ease

        half intense

    waiting for the long wait

to disembark ... finally

    to freedom

like solving a maze

    traversing corridors

        and turns and stairs

    and more corridors and

        down escalators

to reach a series

    of lines ...

    ... everyone waiting with

    passport in hand

        for that precious entry

Welcome to Thailand!

David A. Folds

time passing

slowly

waiting for the first

sundry group of bags

searching for sizes

shapes or colors

none are ours, yet

and more, then more

then some same ones

... again

until first one

then two more

and relief for finally

the fourth is here

cleared to leave

seeking ground trans

... soon inside ... moving

air ... conditioning the humid

... tropical heat

watching Bangkok gradually

reveal its open ... modern

presence ... near the

thruway ... occasionally

giants posing as office

structures

all along the way

the heat of the sun

out from the car

embraces us in a

tropical mode

... into the hotel

us first .. luggage following

slowly check in

... identify

... show passports

... give credit card

get into the elevator ... at last

David A. Folds

in the morning

... the morning

turned around from the night

that the night should be

on the other side

of the globe

our disrupted systems

try to function

try to normalize

have a normal breakfast

or brunch

in the not-evening morning

bright and hot

sidestepping ... often

passing through

narrow sidewalks filled with

food venders ... selling

barbecued and fried

meat and seafood

and spicy tasty thai soups

past all to reach

the up escalator

up to the Skytrain's air-conditioned

third-story transit view

off to the river station

people wait for

the long river-boats

not sure

which is which

until one or two

minutes decides

who can board

… others left to try again

… once aboard

… only luck brings a seat

it's a cheap ride … but

you must be sure of your stop

or be in for a long ride

David A. Folds

moving out almost before

the last ones are on deck

... stepping forward towards the seats

first choices always go

to head-shaven monks

a tall American must just stand

... still with some head-room

below the low roof

and, like that, one can still see

the passing sights on both sides

but, to use a camera,

you really need one of those seats

which will include an occasional

spray of river water

while for every designated stop

the boat is docked

without announcement

quick to exit

step from floating to a

stable base

follow the traffic

of people between

crowded food stalls and

souvenir vendors

until the goal is in sight

the palace area

surrounded by its high

pure white gated walls

steeped in the heat

of an antagonistic sun

enter the first gate

following traffic

to the ticket windows

and through into

the inner grounds

David A. Folds

to the left – the gold gleaming

Phra Sri Ratana Chedi

a conical top starting as a dome

evolving upward as a ringed

lance – width decreasing

upwards

pointing to the heavens

then Phra Mondop to its right and

the Royal Pantheon further right

so – three fraternal triplets –

about the same height

at ground level

three very different styles

from different periods

with statues as elaborate guards

only part of the compound for the

Temple of the Emerald Buddha

history displayed in

mind-blowing images

rich in colors

rich in design and material

it must be said, it must be –

a feast for the eyes and then

for the mind

opposite these three sits

the Chapel – the Ubosot

of the Emerald Buddha

larger - rectangular

elaborately detailed

square columns alternating

between filled gold

and colored mirror tile

rising to a multi-layered

triangle roof

edged with gold serpents

and going in past the columns

the wall is gold-plated

with elaborate patterns

David A. Folds

and inside these walls

past lion guardians of bronze

past doors with mother-of-pearl

resides the revered

Emerald Buddha

clothed in golden costume

sitting in a gold-covered

throne of wood

precious to Thais, Laos, and Cambodians

with the two latter ones believing

it should belong to them

as it has been

or is alleged to have been in

Pataliputtara and

various other Indian cities

– Ceylon – Angkor Wat

– Ayutthaya – Kamphaeng Phet

– Chang Rai – Chang Mai

– Luang Prabang – Lampang

              – Vientiane – Thonburi

                 and finally Bangkok

further along, there is the Grand Palace

        every part of the roof is Thai style

        but below that the style

            is European influenced

mostly, we only see the exterior

inside, especially the Inner Court,

        never allows tourists, outsiders

only the large reception room

        Chakri Maha Prasat

            is open to us visitors

Dusit Maha Prasat Throne Hall

        if seen from above

        has the shape of a cross

        four sections, wings, attached

            to a center with a

            Thai-decorated prasat spire

            nine-tiered

David A. Folds

each wing topped with

four tiers of tiled roof

inside is a throne inlaid with

mother of pearl

all this seen while tolerating

the heat of a blazing sun

every decorative metallic piece

reflecting the intensity

from above

eyes becoming almost glazed

… and then it is too late –

we started too late and

closing time is now upon us

a step still into a bright space

- sun-locked, heat-sparkled

moving forward

towards shade

glazed images streak through

       parched atmosphere

my own lens closed

       trying to avoid the onslaught

I float through it

       an alien thrown into warped time

we exit to the street

       too late for the river boats

best option is a taxi

       – none will use a meter

           from the palace area

the only way is to agree

       on a flat rate – plus tip

we target MBK

       – the locals' shopping mall

       a place for bargains

       – inside escaping the sun

12/23/10 – 07/09/13 - Jersey City, NJ

David A. Folds

Observing

a leaf fallen

    to the ground

… partially curled

turns this way and that

    sometimes spins

    sometimes dances

    … its own ballet

in bits and starts

now with a wind's

    next push

until a next

    intermission

just a small thing

filtered out

by most

... not chosen as worthy

performance on an

outdoor stage

with an audience of one

09/01/13 - Jersey City, NJ

David A. Folds

Disconnected

we walk through

soft places

unaware

life in a quiet pause

absence of impact

thoughts elsewhere

not here, not now

moments separated

from the external

where is the present

when lost in a sea

of floating

meandering

mental threads

life lost in a puzzle

with many missing

pieces

06/08/14 - Jersey City, NJ

　　　David A. Folds

You're Away

when you've been away

for more than

a few days

there is a gap

an empty space

in all my being

that knows that you

are still you

but that you're not here

or even near

now ... that space

stays hollow

feeling dull

and heavy

until once again is filled

when you come home

10/12/14 - Jersey City, NJ

Giving Thanks To Vickie

thanks is given

for the calm

separating the quiet

from the joy

the laughter

from the tears

moments of fullness

from those that seem empty

life with direction

from times of confusion

with simplicity, clarity

found among the chaos

connecting everything

and – I give the most thanks

for all my times

connecting with you

11/27/14 - Jersey City, NJ

David A. Folds

Lost Among the Shade

in the park

the song of the trees

dances to the music

of the sunlight

and the wind

huge shadows and

shafts of light

long brilliant corridors

mixed with static shade

the quiet hums

with patience and

slow tempo

particles – bits of something

or else perhaps nothing

float, alive in the sunlight

but invisible

in the shadows

we are incidental

the accidental

transient witnesses

awash in the lushness

of the park

10/25/14 - Jersey City,

David A. Folds

Spirit

In the younger days

of my inner quest

my spirit soared high

above my physical being

out of body

looking downward

… occasionally

dramatically telling me

that all one's existence

is not contained

in one's body

the vehicle

for this outer journey

was Hindu-based meditation

but, the spirit is broader

than any religion

but any religion or spirituality

on its particular path

can awaken the spirit within

and all the spiritual roads

can lead to Om

– the oneness of everything

1/16/15 - Jersey City, NJ

David A. Folds

Rain

the wind moves the rain

    like a pointillistic river

a true aggression

    without anger

and all life exists between

    the drops

all drops exist between the life

water is the source

    water the sustainer

water is the rebirth

    water the destroyer

now, wash your mind

    your heart, your soul

    in this rain

when the rain begins - softly

    - now larger - more frequent

    - heavy - now almost a deluge

       nothing is dry

we watch the ending

    of the rain

       as though one life

        has passed

    another yet to come

when we finally get dry

5/8/15 - Jersey City, NJ

David A. Folds

Somewhere

somewhere I have never traveled

or seen

or thought of

is a place of quiet beauty

that would beckon

if there were some

connecting point

some other reality that

could pull me towards

its deeper world

its richness remains

I still do hope

somewhere out there

still beyond perception

and my touch

7/21/15 - Jersey City, NJ

149   David A. Folds

The Towers

now, it's fourteen years

    and echoes still haunt my mind

knowing of such precious losses

    brought to us from

        hatred … not from religion

Islam is not about terrorism

… they twist the words of holy men

    justifying irrationality

      their real enemies

    are themselves

lost in the rubble of the towers

were far too many lives

but we, as a people, survive

terror cannot defeat

our righteousness

and hope

these two rise again

like twin towers

ultimately … cornerstones

for the growth of our culture

8/2/15 - Jersey City, NJ

David A. Folds

Bach

hear the song sung

slowly

to mark the heightened moments

of an aria

after a cascading

and then rebuilding

chorus of a chorale

watch the sight

of the sound

in a soprano's face

hear the beauty

in the strength of high

pure power notes

the power in the beauty

of lower bass notes

while the orchestra builds

a communion

with soloists and choir

absorbed in

the majesty of Bach

9/8/15 - Jersey City, NJ

David A. Folds

When I Am Home In My Being

when I am home

    in my being

there is not lost

    nor found

my own strength holds its place

    without opposing another

my mind may float, swiftly,

    over images and ideas

but they flow away ... now past

    quickly ... none taking root

as I refocus the moment

    almost gone before it's here

and my experience

    proceeds

still accumulating

still building

    even more

9/16/15 - Jersey City, NJ

Fall Is Here

the well-tempered

tone of Autumn

spreads its

temporary comforter

heating our visual moments

dropped

already released

waterless leaves

splay out

waiting for

pick-up or a

return to Earth's

elements

while still branched yellow

brown and red

dance in the wafting breeze

and in rays from the sun

the spot-light for this presentation

11/7/15 - Jersey City, NJ

155

David A. Folds

Life In-Between

we reach

    the shores of our being

exhausted

    from the stress of trying

every day at twilight

    the rhythmic tide

        monotonously

        repeats its

            rushes to shore

            wave upon wave

and we look

    out to sea

wondering if

    our future

        will lie grounded

or will it

flounder in the

vastness

of infinite expanse

far beyond our

comprehension

12/1/15 - Jersey City, NJ

David A. Folds

THE 12 SEASONS OF LIFE

From 01/01/04 to - 12/7/15

March - New Spring

a westwind wafts overhead

we crawl aimlessly

    seeking change

the song is sung

    to sooth us

    to soften the unknown

        the harsh insistence of

        evolving interaction

if we survive

    we will grow straight

    geometric expanse caught in a

        calcium-carbon explosion in a

    child's body -- reproducing

        to enlarge into promises

        of similar becomings

who is this starting to climb

    reaching out to everything?

we bring the individuality

    through the all-embracing –

    demanding phase of definition

worldly ignorance

    seeking the knowledge of

    each separateness

        never to capture

        each passing moment

        of spent experience

when will we be one …

    or even two?

01/01/04 - Singapore

161   David A. Folds

April - Spring Growth

we are the children of

    the hot pursuit -- running

    in two directions

what we need and what we want

both demanding -- sometimes

    agreeing – sometimes in conflict

the id strong from birth --

the ego developing --

    imposed on by first external

    and finally internal restraint –

    guidance from the ages

        filtered through imperfect

        parentage – almost a future us

we are more than our future

    and less

we walk with knowledge

    married to the unknown,

        the hidden and the unknowable

promises are certain

    fulfillment only a possibility

boldly we step through

    each darkened vestibule

    to open a new lighted

    pathway of maybes

01/03/04 - Bangkok, Thailand

David A. Folds

May - Spring To Early Summer

when the wind howls

    searching the darkness

wolves retreat

    seeking shelter

    wise as most humans

    delaying most daily needs

but the young

    beyond the age of

        constant care

    challenge even

        the forces of nature

curious to test

    determined to

        extend their power

sometimes finding

    success sometimes failure

reaching out to

    explore possibilities

foolishly fearless

    still partially unbound

    discovery more valued

    than wise safety

elders trying to pull on the reins

04/05/04 - Jersey City, NJ

David A. Folds

June - New Heat in Summer

we were the last

if only for a moment

and the first

dragging childhood ways

not yet discarded

nature has betrayed us

we have no choice ... swimming

in a river

of new discovery

our change is chemical

the change is sexual

we're still the same

but becoming different

... new feelings

... new perceptions

we try to show

    the same self

        we were before

    until accepting

        the new

        challenge the

        portal reached

and walk on through

        … new heat controlling

07/11/04 - Jersey City, NJ

David A. Folds

July - Mid-Summer

It seems the brightest

… heat still expanding

though the day's still early

everything's thought possible

… some already there

… some a future maybe

the energy's intense

sometimes focused

often undirected

with an awareness

of power

but when that power

is absent we

must try to learn

with frustration

to adjust

to imperfection

to draw strength

to compromise

… rebalance

or slide into

a sea

built on confusion

11/25/04 - Jersey City, NJ

David A. Folds

August - Mid To Late Summer

now childhood

is done

but will not die

the smallness of

immediate desires

lingers

trying to control

the world has become wide

but the possibilities

just narrow

the walls and ceilings

... more defined

we're caught

between

what is safe locally

and the need

to pass through

... finding windows

... doors ... a future

beyond this

place in life

if time does not open

doors

... we will

or such chances

will vanish

trapping us

so then

do it

we must

5/8/05 - Jersey City, NJ

David A. Folds

September – Late Summer

in the first

long mid-journey

of life

days pass into weeks

months into years

time to become

like a rock

the foundation of

a small universe

of existence

to maintain to

structure ... to support

a family ... a life force

is now the basis

for each day's struggle

the breadth of what's earned

to care for the home

the growth of the small ones

... care givers to caretakers

choices against freedom

choosing for the future

now is their time

3/8/08 - Jersey City, NJ

173   David A. Folds

October – Autumn

still life is a family

not alone

rarely, can we be alone

routines are constant

and consistent

weekends eased

and slowed down

Saturday -- a softer day

some nights with parties

sometimes given

when owed

Sunday with early commitments

and later options

for afternoon

and dinner

with gathered family

all wrapping around

to Monday's return

to work's insistent patterns

striving to keep tied

life's complex package

12/7/15 - NYC, NY

David A. Folds

November – Late Autumn

we reach milestones

twenty-five

thirty or forty years of work

hopefully years of growth,

upward

hopefully secure

with job and future retirement

we know we have been painted

into patterns

that are predictable

life has little time for creativity

grown children and their children

visit

watch to discover

the secrets of older folk

we are those –

    the older generation

       still working, still ticking

           while life seems to

              go on ever faster

12/7/15 - NYC, NY

177   David A. Folds

December – Early Winter

the world is very changed

from our younger years

modernized,

technicalized,

communication linked

brassy, brash,

lacking peace

we continue within it

somehow,

something like we used to

when we were young

in another age

this is not even

       the children's time

it's becoming

       the children's children's time

retirement is near

       or already here

now we must solve the problem

       how and where to use

       this new free time

12/7/15 - NYC, NY

David A. Folds

January – Winter

we are still slower

slower than those

in their sixties

most days

do not start with a rush

not a deadline

no schedule of working hours

in a community of elders

only the attendants and visitors

are not old

the people share stories

of their earlier

active lives

and gossip about

who has what problem

or who is getting together

with whomever

but the world is spinning

faster than our lives

we wait for when

our world slows even more

12/7/15 - NYC, NY

David A. Folds

February – Late Winter

in the old age home

    we are now the ones

        about whom the others speak

did you hear about her

how is he doing

the younger world

    of doctors and nurses

        and attendants

    are our overseers

        our protectors

TV and other entertainments

try to fill the vacuum of time

between meals

and between sleep

the time of nothingness

anyway, we keep going on

not towards a goal

but continue until the end

12/7/15 - NYC, NY

David A. Folds

Eye Contact

silence spoken swiftly

passes without notice

sound with

spiked decibels

intrudes harshly

streaming through

forcing itself

upon us

the silence is hidden underneath

focused eyes

     suddenly on us

          from a stranger

               or a friend

    hit us heavily

        with silence

    soundlessly

        like spiked decibels

with silence

     echoing in our ears

     but not in our mind

David A. Folds
12/24/15 - Jersey City, NJ

David A. Folds

Index of Poems by Titles

All Light 12

An Eye For Luck 100

Bach 152

Changes 80

Cheap Elevations 20

Closed Doors 110

Cosmic Breaths 92

Dad – a Gift to Us 98

Dances of the Tribe 14

Dark Dreams 106

Darshan 112

Dawning Dusk 34

Disconnected 138

Diversions 16

Duet 10

Ebb Tide 74

Enter Ideas 9

Eternal Moments 33

Eye Contact 184

Fall Is Here 155

Fog 116

Geese 118

Geodesic Oasis 64

Giving Thanks To Vickie 141

Growth and Pain 18

Heat 72

Hiatus 66

In Fellowship 36

Lessons 86

Life In-Between.. 156

Light Years...95

Long Notes 6

Lost Among the Shade 142

Lost in the Web..62

Microbe..78

Minuscule 22

Moment in Mount Laurel.......................................61

Moments 56

Morning Journey..54

My Truth..109

Nibbling Time...42

Now's Revenge 11

Observing 136

Old Isan 88

Old Seasons 44

On Stage 104

Out of the Dark 24

Passage..70

Perception 68

Phases...102

Raptor Rising...120

Rain 146

Rebirth...48

Reflecting Pool 4

Returning 38

River 58

Showers 52

Silence...76

Slow Waters 114

Somewhere 148

Sounds of Change.. 8

Sparrow 40

Spirit 144

Status Quo.. 1

Sweeping By.. 90

The Seasons of Life.. 159

    March - New Spring 160

    April - Spring Growth 162

    May - Spring To Early Summer 164

    June - New Heat in Summer........................ 166

    July - Mid-Summer..................................... 168

    August - Mid To Late Summer 170

    September - Late Summer 172

    October – Autumn...................................... 174

    November - Late Autumn 176

    December - Early Winter 178

    January – Winter.. 180

    February - Late Winter................................ 182

The Towers 150

To Sophia.. 2

To the Core 84

Trips... 122

Two 82

Watching Time 50

When I Am Home In My Being 154

You're Away 140

www.ingramcontent.com/pod-product-compliance
Lightning Source LLC
Chambersburg PA
CBHW021057090426
42738CB00006B/383